ABD-RU-SHIN
THE TEN COMMANDMENTS OF GOD
THE LORD'S PRAYER

D1225858

THE TEN
COMMANDMENTS OF GOD

THE LORD'S PRAYER

EXPLAINED
TO MANKIND
BY
ABD-RU-SHIN

GRAIL·FOUNDATION·PRESS

GAMBIER, OHIO

The Ten Commandments of God and The Lord's Prayer
contains the translation according to the sense
of the original German text. In some cases
the words of the translation can
only render the original meaning approximately.
Nevertheless, the reader will come to a
good understanding if he or she absorbs inwardly
the meaning of the contents.

The Ten Commandments of God and The Lord's Prayer.

Copyright ©1996 by the Stiftung Gralsbotschaft under special license to
Grail Foundation Press, P.O. Box 45, Gambier, Ohio 43022

Original German edition:
Die zehn Gebote Gottes und das Vaterunser

Paperback, eighth edition, 1996.
Only authorized edition.

All rights are reserved in whole or in part concerning translation
and dissemination through public lectures, films, radio, television,
any kind of sound carrier, copying, photographic reproduction, or any other
form of duplication or storage by computer. Reprinting only with
permission of the owners of the copyright.

Library Systems and Services Cataloging-in-Publication Data

Abd-ru-shin, 1875-1941.
[Zehn Gebote Gottes und das Vaterunser. English]
The Ten Commandments of God, the Lord's prayer :
explained to mankind / by Abd-ru-shin.
p. cm.
Translation of: Die zehn Gebote Gottes und das Vaterunser.
ISBN 1-57461-004-X
1. Ten commandments. 2 Lord's prayer..
I. Title. II. Ten commandments of God. III. Title: Lord's prayer
BV4655.A2313 1995   241.5'2—dc20

Printed on recycled paper.

"HE WHO

MAKES NO EFFORT

TO GRASP ARIGHT

THE WORD OF THE LORD

BURDENS HIMSELF

WITH GUILT!"

ABD-RU-SHIN

THE TEN COMMANDMENTS OF GOD

The First Commandment:

I AM THE LORD THY GOD!
THOU SHALT HAVE NO OTHER GODS BUT ME!

He who is able to read these words aright will doubtless already see in them the sentence for many who do not observe this most exalted of all the Commandments.

"Thou shalt have no other gods!"

Many a man reads far too little into these words. He has made it too easy for himself! In the first place he probably thinks of idolaters only as those people who kneel before a row of wooden figures, each one of which represents a particular god; perhaps thinks also of demon-worshippers and others similarly gone astray, at best calling them to mind with pity, but he does not include himself among them.

Just take a look at yourselves calmly for once, and examine yourselves as to whether perchance you belong to them after all!

One has a child who really means more to him than anything, for whom he could make any sacrifice, forgetting all else. Another sets earthly pleasure far above everything, and with the best volition would in the end be absolutely incapable of renouncing this pleasure for anything, if he were faced with such a challenge as afforded him a voluntary decision. A third again loves money, a fourth power, a fifth a woman, another earthly distinction, and again in all these things they all ultimately love only ... themselves!

That is idolatry in the truest sense. The First Commandment warns against it! Forbids it! And woe to him who does not obey it to the letter!

This infringement avenges itself immediately, for such a person must always remain earthbound when he passes over into the Ethereal Realm. In reality however he has only bound himself to the earth through the propensity for something which is upon earth! He is thus held back from further ascent, loses the time given to him for it, and runs the risk of not emerging from the Ethereal Realm in time to rise therefrom to the Luminous Realm of the free spirits.

He will then be swept along into the inevitable disintegration of all material substance, which serves to purify it for *its* resurrection and its new formation. But for the human soul this is spiritual death to all the personal consciousness it had developed, and therewith also the destruction of its form and its name for eternity!

Obedience to this Commandment is meant to give protection from this terrible fate! It is one of the most exalted Commandments, because it remains the one most necessary to man! Unfortunately, he is all too apt to yield to some propensity which finally enslaves him! But whatever he allows to become a propensity he therewith makes into a golden calf, which he sets in the highest place, and thereby also as a false deity or idol beside his God, very often even *above* Him!

Unfortunately there are only too many "propensities" which man has created for himself, and which with the utmost thoughtlessness he readily adopts! A propensity is the predilection for something earthly, as I have already pointed out. Naturally there are still many more of them.

But he who acquires a propensity is "caught", as the word correctly indicates. Thereby he is caught by the gross material when he enters the beyond for his further development, and cannot easily detach himself again from it; he is thus retarded, held back! It can indeed also be called a curse that is a perpetual burden to him. The process is the same, no matter how it is expressed in words.

If in his life on earth, however, he puts God above all else, not only in his imagination or merely in words, but in his intuitive perceiving, thus truly and genuinely, in reverential love that binds him as if to a propensity, then through the binding he will at once strive upwards through the same effect when he enters the beyond; for he takes with him the reverence and love for God; it supports him and finally bears him into Paradise, the abode of the pure spirits who have become free from all burdens, and whose binding leads only to God's Luminous Truth!

Therefore pay strict attention to the keeping of this Commandment. You will be protected thereby from *many* unfavourable threads of fate.

THOU SHALT NOT TAKE THE NAME OF THE LORD THY GOD IN VAIN!

The Name awakens and gathers the concept in man! Whoever dishonours a name and dares to debase it, thereby debases the concept! Bear this in mind at all times!

This clear Commandment of the Lord, however, is the least observed of all the Ten Commandments, thus the most transgressed. This non-observance takes a thousand different forms. Even though man thinks that many of these transgressions are quite harmless, only superficial expressions, nevertheless it remains a transgression of this explicitly given Commandment!

Just these thousandfold forms of allegedly only harmless non-observance degrade the Holy Name of God, and with it the concept of God which is always closely associated with the Name, robbing It of Its Holiness before men, indeed even before children, defiling Its sanctity by making It commonplace, by dragging It down into general phraseology!

Men do not shrink from venturing into the ridiculous with this. Not one of the many expressions will I cite; for the Name is far too high and sublime for that! But anybody need only observe this for even *one* day, and he will probably be aghast at the enormous ac-

cumulation of transgressions of the Second Commandment by human beings of both sexes, among old and
young, right down to children who are hardly able to
form a proper sentence yet. For "like father, like son"!

For this reason the debasing in particular of God is
often one of the first things that young people learn in
the only apparently so harmless transgressions of God's
Laws!

The effect, however, is the worst of all the transgressions! It has spread abroad in an absolutely dev-
astating way among all mankind, not only with Christians, but also among Muslims, among Jews and Budd-
hists; the same can be heard ad nauseam everywhere!

What value, then, can the Name "GOD" still hold
for man! It is debased, is respected not even as much
as the least of all coinage! Much worse than a worn-
out garment. And this man of the earth, otherwise so
would-be-clever, regards it as harmless, and sins in this
more than a hundred times a day!

Where is reflection! Where the least stirring of the
intuitive perception! You, too, have become completely
deadened to it, and listen calmly when the most sacred
of all concepts is thus trampled into the dirt of every-
day life!

But do not be deceived! The debit account in the
beyond is therewith mercilessly charged for each one
who has sinned in this respect! And just this is not so
easy to expiate because it is attended by such far-
reaching ill consequences, which must avenge them-

13

selves unto the third and fourth generation, unless one day there is some person in this chain of descendants who recognises this evil practice and calls a halt to it.

Therefore try to combat the harmful habit in the circle of your acquaintances. But above all first sever your own threads of karma with all the energy you still possess, so that your debit account will not become greater than it is already in this respect. Do not believe that atonement will be easy because hitherto you intended no evil at all with this! The harm is none the less exactly the same! And the sin against the Commandment remains absolutely unchanged! You knew the Commandment perfectly well.

If you did not really strive to become clear about its significance, then that is *your* fault! Nothing can be written off for you on that account either! Listen and act, so that you become capable of redeeming much while still on earth.

Otherwise the morass which awaits you when you enter the beyond, and which places itself obstructively in the path of ascent, will be terrifying.

Yet not only the individual human being, but also the authorities have shown their opposition to this Commandment for centuries, in that they forcibly demanded of human beings the taking of oaths, compelling them to commit the transgression with the threat of earthly punishment if they did not comply with the demand. But the punishment in the beyond is far more severe, and it falls upon all those who exacted the oath, not upon those who had to take it under pressure. Also Christ once more said explicitly:

"Let your communication be yea or nay; for whatsoever is more than these cometh of evil!"

And indeed the authorities had the power to give the decisive weight to the Yes or No by punishing a deception before the court in the same way as perjury ! In this way they were able to raise the value of the words before the court to that level which they needed to give a judgment. It was not necessary to lead people by force to the transgression of God's Commandment on that account!

But the churches and their representatives carried it even further; with invocations to God, they subjected their fellow-men to the most terrible tortures, and with invocations to God they burned them if they had not already succumbed to their torments beforehand.

The Roman Emperor Nero, well known to all and notorious for his cruelty, was not so bad, not so damnable in his tortures of the Christians as many a church with its enormous record of sins in regard to the Laws of God! First, he did not murder and torture nearly so much, and second, not with such hypocritical invocations to God; invocations of this kind must be numbered among the greatest blasphemies which it is possible for a person to perpetrate.

It avails nothing if these same churches today condemn what in those days had unfortunately been perpetrated through them all too long; for they did not voluntarily abandon it!

And even today there is not much difference in the mutual, only more restrained hostility and in another, more modern form! In this, too, only the *form* has changed in the course of time, not the living core! And this core alone, which one so likes to conceal, counts before the Judgment of God, never the outward form!

And this present, only apparently harmless form was born out of the same unspeakable spiritual arrogance of the representatives of *all* the churches, as hitherto. And where this damnable arrogance is not present, there is to be found an empty conceit based on the earthly power of the churches. Often enough these vices result in the most unseemly hostilities, interwoven in addition with earthly calculations towards the extending of influence, if not even towards a hankering after great political importance.

And all this with the Name of "GOD" on their lips, so that I want to call out again like the Son of God: "By your deeds you have stamped my Father's houses, through considering them to be in *your* honour, as dens of murderers! Servants of God's Word you call yourselves, but you have become servants of your own arrogance!"

Every Catholic thinks himself far better before God than a Protestant, without there being any cause for it, but every Protestant thinks himself more enlightened, more advanced, and *thus* nearer to his God than the Catholic! And these are all those who claim to be followers of Christ, to form themselves according to His Word.

Both parties are fools, who rely on something that does not count in the least before the Will of God! Just all these sin far more against the Second Commandment of God than adherents of other religions; for they misuse the Name of God not only with words but through the deed, with their whole manner of living, even in their so-called Divine Service.

To every thinking and closely-observing person they give only a horrible example of meaningless forms and empty thought. Just in the boundless conceit of wishing to make themselves and those around them believe that they already possess a place in Heaven ahead of those of other faiths, they desecrate the concept of God most deeply!

It is not the outward form of church rites, baptism and so much else that matters! The inner man alone has to stand before the Judgment! Remember this, you haughty ones, to whom it has already been announced that on the Day of Judgment, puffed-up, they will proudly set forth with banners and gorgeous raiment to receive their reward joyously. Yet they will never reach the Realm of the Spirit at the foot of God's Throne, because they will receive the reward they deserve before they get there. An icy blast will sweep them away like worthless chaff; for they lack pure humility *within themselves,* and true love for their neighbour!

By their nature they are the worst misusers of the Name of "GOD", the most flagrant transgressors of the Second Commandment!

They all served Lucifer, not God! And thus they scorn all the Commandments of God! From the first to the last! But mainly this Second one, the transgression of which here is the blackest defilement of the concept of God in the Name!

Beware of continuing to pass over this Commandment lightly! From now on, watch yourselves and your surroundings keenly! Reflect that if you faithfully keep nine of the Commandments and disregard one of them, you will *still* be lost in the end!

When a Commandment is given by God, that is already proof that it must not be taken lightly, that it is absolutely imperative for it to be fulfilled! Otherwise it would never have been given to you.

Do not dare to pray if you are unable to vibrate with your whole soul in the words, and beware lest you reveal yourselves as thoughtless prattlers before your God; for thereby you would be guilty before Him of misuse of the Name of God.

Before you ask Him for something, consider carefully whether it is urgently needed! Do not become entangled in formal prayers to be rattled off at certain times, as has become the bad habit in *all* religious practices. This is not only misuse of God's Name but blasphemy!

In joy or need, an ardent intuitive perceiving without words remains far more valuable than a thousand spoken prayers, even if this intuitive perceiving lasts only a fraction of a second. For such intuitive perceiving is then always genuine, and no hypocrisy! Hence never a misuse of the concept of God either.

It is a *sacred* moment when the human spirit wishes to cast itself in supplication or gratitude before the Steps of God's Throne! This must never become habitual chatter! Not by the servants of a church either!

That man who is capable of using the Name of God on every possible and impossible occasion in daily life has never had the faintest idea of the concept of God! As a human spirit he *must* possess the ability to perceive inwardly a divining of God, even though it be but once in his earth-life! But this once alone would suffice to deprive him of every desire to transgress the Second Commandment thoughtlessly! He will then eternally bear within himself the need to utter the Name "GOD" only in the highest purity of his whole inner being!

Whoever does not have this is far removed from even being worthy of God's Word, much less of entering God's Kingdom! Of enjoying His blissful proximity! For this reason it is also forbidden to make a *picture* of God the Father according to man's concepts! Every attempt at this is bound to lead to nothing but a pitiful belittling, since neither the human spirit nor the human hand is enabled to see even the minutest part of the reality in visions, and to retain it in the earthly way in a picture! The greatest work of art in this could signify only deep degradation.

A Single Eye, in Its unutterable radiance, suggests

everything! – *Thus* exalted is the to you inconceivable Greatness which you embrace in the Word "GOD", and which with careless audacity you often dare to use as the most ordinary of empty and thoughtless expressions! You will have to render account of this conduct of yours!

The Third Commandment:

THOU SHALT KEEP THE SABBATH DAY HOLY!

Who takes the trouble to experience a Commandment with his intuitive perception. When one sees how thoughtlessly children and adults habitually treat the Commandments of their God, every serious-minded person could and should be horrified.

The Commandments are learned and superficially discussed at school. A person is happy if he has taken in the words, and can to some extent give answers concerning them, so long as there is any danger of his being questioned about them. When he leaves school to enter public life these words too are soon forgotten, and with them also the meaning. The best proof of the fact that he was not really interested at all in what his Lord and God demands of him.

But He does not even *demand* anything, but *gives* in love to all men what they urgently need! From the Light it was indeed perceived how far human beings were going astray. So, like a teacher, God faithfully showed them the way that leads them to Eternal Life in the Luminous Realm of the Spirit, thus to their happiness. Whereas disobedience must lead to misery and ruin for mankind!

Just for that reason it is not really correct to speak

21

of *Commandments*. Rather they are very well-meant advice, pointing out the right way through the World of Matter, with which the human spirits themselves wished to become acquainted.

But even this so beautiful thought has no effect on man. He has literally become far too obdurate in his own ways of thinking, and will see or hear nothing more than what he himself has put together in the way of views, on the basis of his small earthly knowledge.

He does not perceive how the World of Matter is constantly carrying him further, ever further, right to the boundary where for the last time he is faced with "Either – Or", as *the* decision which now remains decisive for his entire existence, and according to which he must follow his path so chosen to the end, without being able to turn back from it again. Even if finally recognition yet comes to him. It will then be too late, and will only serve to increase the torments for him.

To help in this, so that in spite of the errors recognition could yet come to him *in time,* God gave men the *Third* Commandment, the advice to keep the Sabbath Day holy!

With the fulfilment of this Commandment there would indeed have gradually arisen for every human being in the course of time the longing to strive towards the Light, and with the longing the way would finally also have been revealed that would bring him upwards to the fulfilment of his wishes which, growing ever stronger, would have condensed into prayer. Then man would stand *differently* today! Spiritualised, *mature* for *that* Kingdom which must now come.

Thus hearken *ye,* and act so that fulfilment of the Commandment will prepare your way. You are to keep the Sabbath Day holy! *You!* It states quite clearly in the words that *you* are to consecrate the Sabbath Day, you must make it *holy for yourself!*

The Sabbath Day is the hour of rest, thus when you take rest from the work enjoined upon you by your path on earth. But you do not consecrate the hour of rest, the day of rest, by wishing to care only for your body. Nor by seeking diversion in games, drinking or dancing.

The hour of rest should lead you to hold quiet self-communion in your thinking and intuitive perceiving, to review your earth-life up to the present, especially always the past working days of the *last* week, and to draw practical applications from them for your future. Six days can always be reviewed; a longer period is easily forgotten.

Inevitably then your intuitive perceiving will slowly rise higher, and you will become a seeker for the Truth. Once you really are a seeker, a way will also be shown to you. And just as here on earth you only tread a new, hitherto unfamiliar path with care, investigating it, so must you cautiously proceed step by step also on the new spiritual paths which open before you, in order always to keep firm ground under your feet. You must not rush ahead, for then the danger of falling is greater.

Through such thinking and intuitive perceiving during the rest hours of your earth-life you will never lose anything, but only gain.

No one keeps an hour of rest holy by going to church, unless at the same time during the time of rest he is prepared to reflect on what he has heard there, in order to absorb it rightly within himself and live accordingly. The priest cannot make your day holy for you if you do not do so of yourself. Consider carefully ever again whether the real sense of the Word of God is completely in accord with your activity. Through *this* way the Sabbath Day will then be kept holy by you; for through peaceful self-communion it has acquired *that* content for the purpose of which it was instituted.

Every Sabbath Day will thus become a milestone on your way, which will also retroactively give the days of your gross material activity *that* value which these should have for the maturing of your soul. Then they will not have been lived in vain, and you will constantly advance.

To keep holy means not to waste. The moment you neglect this you lose the time which is granted to you for maturing, and after the Cosmic Turning-Point, the rays of which are now slowly encompassing you, only a short time is yet given to make up for what has been neglected, provided that in so doing you use all the energy left to you.

Therefore keep the Sabbath Day holy! Be it in

your home, or better still in Nature, which helps you to become alert in thinking and intuitive perceiving! Fulfil thereby the Commandment of the Lord. It is for *your* benefit!

The Fourth Commandment:

THOU SHALT HONOUR FATHER AND MOTHER!

God had this Commandment given to mankind. But it has caused unspeakable anguish of soul. How many a child, how many an adult, has struggled desperately not to offend most grossly against just this Commandment.

How can a child honour the father who degrades himself to the level of a drunkard; or a mother who grievously embitters the hours of the father and the entire household through her caprices, through her unrestrained temper, lack of self-discipline and so much else, making a peaceful atmosphere quite impossible!

Can a child honour its parents when it hears them roundly abusing and deceiving each other, or even coming to blows? How many a conjugal incident has often made the Commandment a torment for the children, rendering it impossible of fulfilment.

In the long run it would indeed be nothing but hypocrisy if a child were to assert that it still honoured a mother when she behaves in a much more friendly way towards strangers than towards her own husband, the child's father. When it observes with her the propensity to superficiality, sees her sink in the most ridiculous vanity to a weak-minded slave of every fashionable craze, which so often can no longer be associated with the concept of earnest, high motherhood, and which robs motherly dignity of all beauty and sublimity ... on what is a child then still to base voluntary reverence for its mother? What indeed lies in the one word: "Mother!" But also what does it demand.

A child that is not yet contaminated as well *must* unconsciously sense within that a person of mature, serious spirit can never set out to expose her physical body merely for the sake of fashion. How then can the mother remain sacred to the child! Natural reverence impulsively sinks down to the empty form of a habitual duty or, depending upon the upbringing, to self-evident conventional politeness, thus to hypocrisy, which lacks all upward swinging of the soul. Just *that* upward swinging which holds warm life! Which is indispensable to a child, and accompanies him like a secure shield as he grows up and sets out in life, guarding him against temptations of all kinds, and remaining inwardly a strong tower of refuge for him, whenever doubts of any kind assail him. Right up to old age!

The word "mother" or "father" should at all times call forth a warm, fervent intuitive perception out of which the image arises before the soul in full purity, *dignified*, warning or assenting, as a guiding star throughout his entire earthly existence!

And what a treasure is now taken from every child when it *cannot* honour its father or its mother with its whole soul!

Yet the cause of these agonies of soul is again only men's false interpretation of the Commandment. The hitherto-prevailing view was wrong; it limited the meaning and allowed it to become one-sided, whereas surely nothing sent by God can be one-sided.

But it was still more wrong that this Commandment was distorted, in that it was to be improved according to human estimation, made still more explicit by an addition: "Thou shalt honour *thy* father and *thy* mother!" In this way it became personal. This was bound to lead to errors; for the Commandment in its right form is only: "Thou shalt honour father and mother!"

Hence it does not refer to particular, specific persons, whose *nature* cannot be determined and foreseen from *the outset.* Such a paradox never occurs in the Divine Laws. On no account does God demand that something be honoured which does not also absolutely deserve to be honoured!

On the contrary, this Commandment embraces a *concept* of fatherhood and motherhood instead of personality. Therefore it is not in the first place addressed to the children but to the *parents* themselves, demanding of *them* that they keep fatherhood and motherhood in honour! The Commandment imposes absolute duties upon parents, always to be fully conscious of their high task, and therewith also to bear in mind the responsibility involved in it.

In the beyond and in the Light one lives not with words but in concepts.

For this reason it happens that in rendering these concepts in words it is easy for a limitation to occur, as becomes obvious in this case. But woe unto those who have not respected this Commandment, who have not taken the trouble to recognise it aright. It is no excuse that hitherto it has so often merely been misinterpreted and wrongly apprehended.

The consequences of not keeping the Commandment made themselves felt even with procreation and the entry of the soul. It would be quite different on this earth if the incisive Commandment had been understood and fulfilled by men. Quite different souls could then have incarnated, who would have been incapable of permitting a corruption of morality and ethics to such a degree as exists today!

Just look at the murdering, look at the wild dances, look at the orgies into which everything today tends to develop. The crowning, as it were, of the triumph of sultry currents of the Darkness. And look at the uncomprehending indifference with which the decline is accepted, and even encouraged as something that is right or that has always been in existence.

Where is the man who takes the trouble to recognise the Will of God aright, who, swinging himself upwards, seeks to grasp the vast magnitude, instead of ever and ever again stubbornly compressing this great Will into the wretched limitation of the earthly brain, which he has made the temple of the intellect. He himself thereby forces his gaze to the ground, like a slave who walks in chains, instead of lifting it upwards, expanding it with radiant joy to meet the ray of recognition.

Do you not see in what a pitiful position you place yourselves with *every* interpretation of all that comes to you out of the Light! Whether it be Commandments, the Promises, the Message of Christ, or indeed the whole of Creation! Nothing will you see, nothing will you recognise! Indeed you do not at all seek *really* to understand a thing! You do not take it as it is, but try convulsively ever again to reshape everything into the inferior views to which you have surrendered yourselves for thousands of years.

Do at last free yourselves from these traditions. The power to do so is certainly at your disposal. Every moment. And without your having to make sacrifices. But they must be thrown off with *one heave,* with *one* act of will! Without trying to retain anything of it. As soon as you try to find a *transition* you will never become free of what has hitherto prevailed, but it will ever again tenaciously drag you back. It can only be easy for you if you sever all the old with *one* slash, and thus step before the new without any old burden. Only then will the gate open to you; otherwise it will remain fast shut.

And that requires only one really serious volition, it is the happening of a moment. Just like awakening from sleep. If you do not then rise at once from your bed you become tired again, and joy in the new day's work flags, if it is not altogether lost.

Thou shalt honour father and mother! Make this now a sacred Commandment for yourselves. Raise fatherhood and motherhood to honour! Who today still knows what great dignity lies in them. And what power to ennoble mankind! Those human beings who unite here on earth should for once be clear about this; then every marriage will really be marriage, anchored in the spiritual! And all fathers and mothers *worthy of honour* according to the Divine Laws!

For children, however, this Commandment will become sacred and living through their parents. They will simply be unable to do anything other than honour father and mother from their soul, regardless of the individual nature of these children. Indeed the very quality of their parents will compel them to do so.

And then woe unto *those* children who do not absolutely fulfil the Commandment. A heavy karma would fall upon them; for there would be ample cause for it. But in the reciprocal action obedience soon becomes a matter of course, a joy and a need! Therefore go forth and heed the Commandments of God more earnestly than hitherto! That means, observe and fulfil them! So that you will become happy! –

The Fifth Commandment:

THOU SHALT NOT KILL!

Yes, beat your chest, O man, and loudly give praise that you are no murderer! For to kill is surely to murder, and according to your conviction you have never transgressed this Commandment of the Lord. Proudly you can step before Him, and without fear and anxiety look hopefully forward to the opening of this particular page in your Book of Life.

But in this connection have you ever considered that for you there is also a *deadening*, and that to *deaden* means the same as to kill?

There is no difference between them. You make it solely in your manner of expression, in your language; for the Commandment does not one-sidedly say: Thou shalt kill no gross material earth-life! But in a great, comprehensive, brief way: Thou shalt not kill!

For example, a father had a son. Petty ambition drove the father to insist that his son should study, at all costs. But this son possessed gifts that urged him to do something else, for which studying would be of no use to him at all.

So it was quite natural that inwardly the son felt no inclination for these enforced studies, nor was he able joyfully to summon up the energy. But the father demanded obedience, and the son obeyed. At the expense of his health he exerted himself to comply with his father's will. But since it was against the son's nature, against the gifts he bore within him, it was quite natural that his body also suffered under it.

I will not pursue the case here any further; it is so often repeated in earthly life. But it is irrefutable that through his ambition or obduracy the father here sought to deaden something in this son which was given to the son to be developed on earth! In many cases it turns out that it is actually deadened, since its development in later life is then scarcely still possible, because the healthy main strength for it has been broken down in its prime, wantonly dissipated on things alien to the boy's nature.

Now the father thereby committed a severe offence against the Commandment: Thou shalt not kill! Quite apart from the fact that by his action he deprived men of something which could perhaps have been of great benefit to them through the boy! However, he must consider that although the boy is or can be spiritually related to him or to the mother, nevertheless before the Creator he remains a personality of his own, whose *duty* it is to develop for his own benefit the gifts he received on coming to earth.

Perhaps through the Grace of God it was thereby also granted to the boy to redeem a heavy karma, in that he was meant to invent something which in a certain sense would bring great benefit to mankind!

This guilt of prevention weighs all the more heavily upon the father or upon the mother who set their petty earthly views above the great threads of fate, and thereby abused their parental power.

It is no different when parents are capable of allowing the paltry earthly calculations of their intellect to predominate in connection with their children's marriages. How often is a most noble intuitive perception of their child ruthlessly stifled thereby, when the child may indeed be given freedom from earthly cares, but with it a distress of soul which remains more incisive for the existence of the child than all the money and earthly possessions.

Naturally the parents should not indulge every dream or wish of a child. That would not be fulfilling their parental duty. But serious examination is demanded, which must never be one-sided in the earthly sense! Just this examination in a *selfless* way, however, is seldom or never applied by parents.

Thus there are cases of a thousand kinds. It is not necessary for me to say any more about it. Ponder over it yourselves, so that you do not transgress this so weighty Word of God in the Commandment! In so doing undreamed-of paths will open to you!

Yet the child can also stifle hopes of its parents which are justified! If it does not develop the gifts within as is necessary in order to achieve great things, once the parents have helpfully allowed the child to choose the path it asked for. Then, too, noble intuitive perceptions are destroyed in its parents, and it has grossly transgressed the Commandment!

Also when a man in some way disappoints the true friendship or confidence that someone gives him. He therewith kills and injures in the other person something which really harbours life! It is transgression of God's Word: Thou shalt not kill! Brings him evil fate, which he must atone for.

You see that all the Commandments are only the best friends for men, to protect them faithfully from evil and from suffering! Therefore love them and respect them as a treasure, the guarding of which brings you only joy! –

The Sixth Commandment:

THOU SHALT NOT COMMIT ADULTERY!

The very fact that there is another Commandment which reads: "Do not let thyself lust after thy neighbour's wife!" shows how little this Sixth Commandment corresponds in meaning to what the earthly law decrees about it.

"Thou shalt not commit adultery" can also read "Thou shalt not break the peace of a marriage!" By peace one naturally understands also harmony. That at the same time stipulates *what* a marriage should really be like; for where there is nothing to break or to disturb, the Commandment, which is not governed by earthly interpretations and regulations but by the Divine Will, does not apply either.

Hence a marriage only exists where harmony and peace reign as a matter of course. Where one always seeks to live only for the other and make him happy. One-sidedness and the so often tempting, deadening boredom are then completely and for ever excluded from the outset, as well as the dangerous craving for distraction or the illusion of being misunderstood! Murder weapons for all happiness!

These particular evils simply *cannot* arise in a proper marriage where the one really lives for the other, because the idea of being misunderstood, and also the craving for distraction, are merely the consequences of a marked selfishness which seeks to live only for itself, but not for the other!

Where there is true love of soul, however, the mutual glad giving up of self is something quite natural, and in this way any disadvantage to one party is reciprocally also quite impossible. Provided that also the degree of culture of those uniting does not show too great a gap!

That is a condition required by the Law of the Attraction of Homogeneous Species in the great Universe, which must be complied with if happiness is to be complete.

But where that peace, that harmony are not to be found, the marriage does not deserve to be called marriage; for then it is not one either, but merely an earthly partnership which as such obtains no value before God, and therefore cannot bring *that* kind of blessing which is to be expected in a true marriage.

Hence with the Sixth Commandment real marriage according to the Will of God is a prerequisite! No other marriage is protected. But woe unto him who dares to disturb a *true* marriage in any way! For the triumph which he imagines he has from it here on earth awaits him ethereally in quite a different form! He would fain flee from it in terror, when he has to cross into the realm where the consequences of his deeds await him.

It is adultery in the most far-reaching sense even

where the attempt is made to separate two souls who really love one another, as is often done by parents when some earthly circumstance or other is not in accordance with their wish!

And woe also to the woman, woe to a man, be they young or old, who out of envy or flirtatiousness consciously brings discord or even strife between such a couple!

Pure love between two human beings shall be hallowed before every one; it shall inspire him with reverence and respect, but not desire! For it stands under the protection of God's Will!

If a feeling of such unclean desire seeks to arise in a human being, then he should turn away and look with clear eyes only among *those* people who have not yet attached themselves to another soul.

If he seeks earnestly and with patience, he will unfailingly also find a person who is suited to him in the way willed by God, with whom he will then also be happy without first burdening himself with some guilt, which can never bring and grant any happiness!

The great mistake of these people is often simply that they go out of their way to yield to a pressure of feeling which to begin with is always weak, retaining it forcibly within them, tending it with artificial fantasy until, gaining strength, it fills them, and tormenting them, drives them also to sin!

Thousands of human spirits would not have to be lost if only they would always pay heed to the *be-*

ginning of it, which, if it is not created by intellectual calculation, merely arises from a flirtatiousness unworthy of a human being, which in turn has its origin in pernicious practices of earthly family and particularly social life! Just these are often nothing but marriage markets, no cleaner than the open slave-trade of the Orient! In them lies a breeding-place for the germs of adultery.

You parents, be on your guard lest you become guilty of adultery in regard to your children, by being too intellectually calculating! Countless parents are already so entangled! It takes much for them to free themselves again from it!

You children, be careful that you do not perhaps become peace-breakers between your parents, or else you too will be guilty of adultery! Ponder this well. Otherwise you make yourselves enemies of your God, and there is no such enemy who would not eventually have to fall to destruction in unspeakable torments, without God lifting a finger!

You must never destroy the peace and the harmony between two human beings. Hammer this into yourself, so that it may always stand as a warning before the eyes of your soul. –

The Seventh Commandment:

THOU SHALT NOT STEAL!

A thief is regarded as one of the most despicable of creatures. A thief is anyone who takes something that belongs to another without his consent!

Therein lies the explanation. To obey this Commandment rightly, a man need do nothing more than always distinguish clearly what belongs to the other person! That is not difficult, everyone will say to himself at once. And with that he has already dismissed the matter.

Certainly, it is not difficult, just as it is not really difficult to obey all the Ten Commandments, if one genuinely wishes to do so. But there always remains the condition that man knows them properly. And it is *this* that many lack.

In order to obey this Commandment, have you ever really considered what actually is the property of another, from which you must not take anything?

There is his money, jewellery, clothes, perhaps also a house and farm, with cattle and all that goes with it. But the Commandment does not state that it concerns only gross material, earthly goods! Indeed, there are values far more precious still!

A man's property includes also his reputation, the

esteem in which he is held in public, his thoughts, his individuality, as well as the confidence he enjoys from others, if not from all yet at least from this or that person!

Once having got so far, many a proud soul will already become rather less confident about the Commandment. For ask yourself: Have you never yet attempted, perhaps in good faith, to shake or completely undermine in another the confidence a person enjoys by a warning to be careful? If so, you have quite literally robbed the one in whom this confidence was reposed! For you have taken it from him! Or at least attempted to do so.

You have also robbed your neighbour if you know something of his circumstances and pass on this knowledge *without the permission of the one concerned.* You can recognise from this how gravely entangled in the meshes of guilt are all those people who seek to make a business out of such things, or who carry on business in this way.

Through all the effects of this activity of continuous transgressions of the Laws of God, the self-entanglements therein draw after them a net so enormous that these people will never again be able to free themselves; for often they are *more heavily burdened* than gross material burglars and thieves. Guilty, and akin to receivers of stolen goods, are those who support and encourage such "businessmen" in their sinful transactions.

Every upright and honourable man, whether private individual or businessman, has the right and the duty to demand an explanation and, if necessary, credentials *direct* from anyone who comes to him with some request, whereupon he can decide how far he can trust him and comply with his wishes. All else is unsound and reprehensible.

Fulfilment of this Commandment has at the same time the further effect of awakening the intuitive perception more and more, and of developing, setting free, its abilities. Man thereby obtains the right knowledge of human nature, which he lost only out of indolence. He gradually loses what is dead, mechanical, and himself becomes once more a living human being. Genuine personalities arise, whereas the herd-animal that is bred today must disappear.

Take the trouble to reflect about this, and see to it that in the end you do not after all find in the pages of your ledger just this Commandment much transgressed!

THOU SHALT NOT BEAR FALSE WITNESS AGAINST THY NEIGHBOUR!

If you assault one of your neighbours and beat him so that he suffers injury, perhaps robbing him as well, then you know that you have harmed him and will become subject to earthly punishment.

But then you give no thought yet to the fact that at the same time you are also entangled in the threads of a reciprocal working which is not subject to any arbitrary action, but which operates justly even to those minute stirrings of your soul to which you pay no heed at all, and for which you have no intuitive perception whatever!

And this reciprocal action is not in the least connected with the earthly punishment, but works quite independently and silently by itself, yet so inescapably for the human spirit that in all Creation he no longer finds any place which can protect and hide him.

When you hear of such a brutal assault and violent injury you are indignant. If people close to you suffer under it you are even alarmed and horrified! Yet it disturbs you little if now and then you hear an absent person being put in a bad light by another through clever malicious words, or often just through very expressive gestures, which imply more than can be said in words.

43

But bear in mind: A gross material attack is far easier to redress than an attack on the soul, which suffers through the undermining of its reputation.

Therefore avoid all scandalmongers as you would gross material murderers!

For they are just as guilty and very often even worse! As little as they take pity on the souls they themselves hound, so little will a helping hand be offered to them in the beyond when they plead for it! Cold and merciless is the pernicious urge in their inner being to discredit others, frequently even strangers to them; coldness and mercilessness a hundred times greater will therefore confront them in that place which awaits them when one day they must leave their physical bodies!

In the beyond they will remain the outlaws and deeply despised, even in the eyes of robbers and thieves; for all their kind have a malicious and despicable feature in common, from a so-called gossip to the depraved creatures who do not shrink from bearing false witness on oath, by their own wish, against a neighbour to whom they have had reason to be grateful in many things!

Treat them as you would poisonous vermin; for they have not deserved otherwise.

Since all mankind completely lack the high, united goal of attaining to the Kingdom of God, they have nothing to say to each other when at times they are together in twos or threes, and so they cultivate talking about others as a habit which has become dear to them, the meanness of which they are no longer able to perceive, because through constantly indulging in it the concept of it has been completely lost.

In the beyond they shall continue to sit together and indulge in their favourite topic until the time granted for the last possibility of ascent, which could perhaps have brought them salvation, has gone by, and they are drawn into eternal disintegration, in which all gross material and ethereal kinds of matter come to purification from *every* poison brought into them by human spirits who are not worthy to retain a name!

DO NOT LET THYSELF LUST AFTER THY NEIGHBOUR'S WIFE!

This Commandment is directed sharply and clearly against the physical-animal instincts which ... alas ... man only too readily allows to arise the moment an opportunity for it is offered him!

Here we have also touched immediately upon the salient point, which forms the greatest snare for human beings, to which almost all succumb as soon as they only come in contact with it: *The opportunity!*

The instinct is merely awakened and guided by the thoughts! Man can very easily observe with himself that the instinct does not stir, cannot stir when the thoughts for it are lacking! It is entirely dependent upon them! Without exception!

Do not say that also the sense of touch can awaken instinct; for that is wrong. It is only a delusion. The sense of touch awakens only the thought, and this in turn the instinct! And in order to awaken thoughts for it, the opportunity that presents itself is the strongest aid, which men must fear!

For this reason, however, it is also the greatest defence and the greatest protection for all human beings of both sexes to avoid the *opportunity* for it! It is the sheet-anchor in the present distress, until all mankind have become so strong in themselves that they are able *to keep the hearth of their thoughts pure* as a healthy matter of course. Then a transgression of the Commandment will be absolutely impossible.

Until then many purifying storms will have to rage over mankind, but *that* anchor will hold if every striving person makes an earnest effort never to give an opportunity for two persons of opposite sex to be alone together, which is so tempting!

Let each one impress this upon his memory in letters of flame; for it is not so easy to free one's soul again from the transgression, since the other party is also involved! And only seldom is it possible to ascend *simultaneously*.

"Do not let thyself lust after thy neighbour's wife!" By this is meant not only a married woman, but the female sex in general! Thus also the daughters! And since it is clearly stated, "Do not let thyself *lust!*", the reference is merely to the physical instinct, not to an honourable wooing!

There can be absolutely no mistake about these clear words. Here it is a matter of the stern Law of God against seduction or rape. As well as of defilement through thoughts of a secret desire! Even this, as the starting-point of the full evil of a deed, is transgression of the Commandment, bringing punishment in its wake through a karma which in some way or other has indispensably to be redeemed before the soul can again be free from it.

This happening, which human beings mistakenly consider a small matter, is sometimes even decisive for the nature of the next incarnation on earth, or for his subsequent fate in *this* earth-life. Therefore do not take too lightly the power of thought, the responsibility for which naturally attaches in like measure! You are answerable for the smallest, most careless thinking; for it causes harm even in the Ethereal World. *That* world which has to receive you after this earth-life.

But if the lusting goes even as far as seduction, thus to a gross material deed, then you may well fear the retribution if you are no longer able to atone for it physically and psychically on earth!

Whether the seduction took place in the most flattering way or by harsh demand, even if the woman's consent was finally won, the reciprocal action will not be turned aside thereby; it has already set in with the desire, and all shrewdness, all artfulness will only serve to *aggravate its effect.* The ultimate consent does not then cancel it!

Therefore be on your guard, avoid every opportunity, and do not give way to any carelessness in this matter! *Above all, keep the hearth of your thoughts pure!* Then you will never violate this Commandment!

Nor will it serve as an excuse if a man seeks to persuade himself that there was the likelihood of marriage! For such a thought would be the very acme of falsehood.

A marriage without love of the soul is not valid in

the sight of God. Love of the soul, however, remains the best protection against infringement of this Commandment; for one who truly loves always wills only what is best for the loved one, and therefore can never make unclean wishes or demands, against which this Commandment is above all directed!

THOU SHALT NOT COVET THY NEIGHBOUR'S HOUSE, NOR HIS FARM, NOR HIS CATTLE, NOR ANYTHING THAT IS HIS!

He who seeks to earn a living through honest work and honest business dealing can look forward calmly to the proclamation of this Commandment during the Great Reckoning, for it will pass him by without striking him a blow. Actually it is so easy to fulfil all the Commandments, and yet ... just look at all men *in the right way*, and soon you will come to recognise that even the keeping of this Commandment, which should really be quite natural for man, is not carried out, or only very seldom, and then not with joy, but only with much effort.

It is as though an unquenchable craving rages over all men, whether white, yellow, brown, black or red, to begrudge his fellow-creatures what he himself does not possess. Still better expressed, however: To envy him everything! In this envy lies already the forbidden coveting! Transgression of the Commandment is thus already complete, and becomes the root of many evils that quickly cause man's downfall, from which he frequently never rises again.

The average man, strange to say, rarely values what he calls his own, but always only that which he does not yet possess. The Darkness assiduously scattered greed, and the human souls, alas, yielded only too willingly, so as to prepare the most fertile soil for the woeful seed.

So with the greater part of mankind, coveting the possessions of others became in time the basis of all their activities. Beginning with a simple wishing, becoming aggravated through cunning and the art of persuasion, to the boundless envy of continual discontent, and even to blind hatred.

Any and every means of gratification was recognised as perfectly fair, provided it did not all too flagrantly conflict with earthly law. In the growing mania for acquisition God's Commandment remained unheeded! Each one considered himself really honourable as long as he was not called to account by an earthly court. To avoid this, however, cost him no great effort, for he applied the utmost circumspection and keenest intellectual cleverness when it was his intention ruthlessly to injure his fellow-men, as soon as it became necessary in order to obtain some cheap advantage for himself.

It did not occur to him that in reality just this costs him far more dearly than all earthly resources can benefit him! So-called cleverness became everything! But cleverness according to *present-day* concepts is in itself nothing more than the blossom of cunning, or an intensification of it. It only remains strange that everyone meets the cunning person with distrust, but the clever one with respect! It is the general *basic attitude* which brings out the inconsistency!

The cunning man is a bungler in the art of gratifying his desire, while intellectually clever people have become masters of it. The bungler cannot clothe his intentions in attractive forms, and reaps only pitying contempt for this. But the most envious admiration flows to the adept from souls who indulge in the same propensity!

Envy also here, because on the soil of present-day humanity even admiration for the same kind cannot be without envy. Men do not know this powerful mainspring of the many evils; they no longer even realise that this envy in many different forms controls and guides all their thoughts and actions at the present time! It has its seat in the individual as in whole peoples; states are guided by it; it engenders wars as well as factions, and unending strife, even where only two persons have to confer about something!

What has become of obedience to the Tenth Commandment of God, one would fain call out warningly to the *states!* In the most merciless greed each one of the earthly states strives only for what the other possesses! In so doing they shrink neither from individual murder nor from mass murder, nor from enslaving entire peoples, only in order to raise themselves to greatness thereby! The fine speeches about self-preservation or self-defence are only evasions, because they themselves feel distinctly that something must be said in order somewhat to mitigate, to excuse these monstrous crimes against the Commandments of God!

But it avails them nothing; for inexorable is the

stylus that engraves disobedience to the Commandments of God in the Book of the World Happening; unbreakable are the threads of karma which thereby attach themselves to each individual, so that not even the slightest stirring of his thinking and doing can be lost without being atoned for!

He who is able to survey all these threads will see what a terrible judgment has now been evoked thereby! Confusion and the collapse of what has been built up until now are only the first *mild* consequences of this most shameful of the violations of the Tenth God-Commandment! As soon as the full effect now begins increasingly to overwhelm you, no one can show you any mercy. You have not deserved otherwise. With this comes only what *you* have forced upon yourselves!

Tear the ignoble coveting completely out of your soul! Consider that a state, too, is only made up of individuals! Eschew all envy, the hatred towards *those* people who in your opinion possess much more than you yourselves! Indeed, there is a reason for it! But the full blame for your inability to recognise that reason is *yours alone,* in that you have voluntarily forced upon yourselves the enormous limitation of your ability to comprehend, which was *not* willed by God, and which is bound to appear as the consequence of your wretched adulation of the intellect!

Whoever in the new Kingdom of God here on earth does not wish to be content with the position given to him, through the working out of his own threads of karma brought about by himself, is not worthy to live in it either! Not worthy of being given therewith the opportunity to atone with comparative ease for old burdens of guilt clinging to him, and at the same time also to mature spiritually, so as to find the way upwards to the home of all *free* spirits, there, where only light and joy reign!

In future every malcontent will be relentlessly snatched away as a useless disturber of the ultimately-willed peace, as a hindrance to healthy ascent! But if there is still within him a germ of good, with a strong promise of an early turning-back, then he will come to recognise the absolute rightness of the wise Will of God; *rightness also for him,* who only out of the short-sightedness of his soul and out of self-willed stupidity could not recognise that the bed in which be *now* lies on earth was solely of his own making, as the absolute consequence of his *entire* existence hitherto, of *several* lives in the beyond and also on earth, but that it is not the blind arbitrary result of chance!

Then he will at last recognise that he needs for himself precisely that and *only* that which he experiences and where he stands, also the circumstances into which he was born, and all that goes with them!

If he works diligently on himself he will mount upwards spiritually, as well as in the earthly sense. However, if he defiantly wants to force a different path for himself, ruthlessly and to the detriment of his fellowmen, then this can never bring him any true benefit.

It will be a hard struggle for the human souls before they are able to free themselves from the habitual transgressions of the Tenth God-Commandment, that is, change themselves in this respect, in order at last really to live in accordance with it in thought, word and in the deed! But suffering and destruction, here on earth and in the beyond, await all those who are unable to do so!

THE LORD'S PRAYER

There are only few human beings who seek to become aware of *what* they actually want when they say the "Lord's Prayer". Still fewer who really know what is the *meaning* of the sentences which they rattle off. Rattle off is probably the only accurate designation for the process which in this instance man calls praying.

He who examines himself unsparingly in this respect *must* admit this, otherwise he proves that he spends his whole life in the same way ... superficially, and that he is not, nor ever has been, capable of any deep thought. There are enough of them on this earth who certainly take themselves seriously, but with the best will in the world cannot be taken seriously by others.

Especially the beginning of this Prayer has always been taken in the wrong sense, even though in different ways. Those who try to undertake this Prayer earnestly, thus who set about it with a certain good volition, experience a certain feeling of safety, of psychic calm arising within them after or during these first words! And this feeling prevails with them for several seconds after praying.

This explains two things: First, that the one who prays can maintain his earnestness only for the first

59

words, whereby they release this feeling in him; and second, that just the release of this feeling proves how far removed he is from grasping what he is saying with them!

In this he plainly shows either his inability to maintain any deeper thinking, or else his superficiality; for otherwise with the succeeding words there should again immediately arise a *different* feeling, corresponding to the changed content of the words, as soon as these really come to life in him.

Thus there persists in him only what the first words awaken. But if he were to grasp the right sense and the true meaning of the words, then these would have to release in him a quite different intuitive sensing from that of being comfortably safe.

More arrogant people again see in the word "Father" the confirmation that they are directly descended from God, and that thereby with the right development they will ultimately themselves become Divine; but that even now they definitely bear something of the Divine within them. And so there are many more errors among men with regard to this sentence.

Most people, however, consider it simply as the *form of address* in the Prayer, the invocation! This requires them to think least. And accordingly it is also uttered without thought, despite the fact that just in the invocation to God should lie the whole fervour of which a man's soul can ever become capable.

But this first sentence is not meant either to say or to be any of this; instead the Son of God at the same time put into the choice of words the explanation or indication *of the way in which a human soul* is to set about prayer, *how* it may and must step before its God if its prayer is to find a hearing. He says exactly what quality it must possess at that moment, how its condition of pure intuitive perception has to be, if it would lay its petition at the Steps of God's Throne.

Thus the whole Prayer is divided into three parts. The first part is the complete dedication, the surrendering of the soul to its God. Figuratively speaking, it bares itself before Him ere it comes with a request, testifying first to its own pure volition.

The Son of God wishes to explain thereby what kind of intuitive perception alone may form the basis for an approach to God! Therefore come, like a great, sacred vow, the words at the beginning: "OUR FATHER, WHO ART IN HEAVEN!"

Consider that prayer is not the same as petition! Otherwise there would certainly be no prayer of thanksgiving, which contains no petition. To pray is not to beg. Even in this respect the "Lord's Prayer" has so far always been misunderstood, because of man's evil habit of never approaching God without at the same time expecting or even demanding something from Him; for in the expecting lies the demanding. And actually man *always* expects something when he prays; this he cannot deny! Be it even, broadly speaking, only the vague feeling of one day receiving a place in Heaven.

Jubilant thanksgiving in happy enjoyment of the

conscious existence granted to him in the co-operation willed by God, or justly expected by God, in the great Creation, for the welfare of his surroundings, is not known to man! Indeed, he does not even suspect that just this, and *only* this, holds his own real welfare and his progress, his ascent.

But on such a basis, willed by God, does the "Lord's Prayer" in truth stand! The Son of God, Who desired only man's welfare, which lies solely in the right observance and fulfilment of God's Will, could not possibly have given it in any other way!

The Prayer given by Him is thus anything but a prayer of petition; rather is it a great, all-embracing vow of man, who in it lays himself at the Feet of his God! Jesus gave it to His disciples, who at that time were ready to live in the pure worship of God, to serve God through their life in Creation, and in this serving to honour His Holy Will!

Man should consider well and carefully whether he may dare to make use of and utter this Prayer at all, and should examine himself earnestly as to whether, in using it, he is not perhaps trying to lie to his God!

The introductory sentences admonish plainly enough that each one should examine himself as to whether he really is as he speaks in it! Whether he dares to go with it before God's Throne without guile!

But if you experience the first three sentences of the Prayer within you, then they will lead you before the Steps of God's Throne. *They are the way to It,* if they come to experiencing in a soul! No other leads thither. But this one for certain! Where these sentences are not experienced, however, none of your petitions can reach there.

It shall be a devout yet joyful outcry when you dare to say: "Our Father, Who art in Heaven!"

In this cry lies your sincere affirmation: "To Thee, O God, I give all a father's rights over me, to which I wish to submit humbly like a child! In doing so I also acknowledge Thine Omniscience, O God, in all that Thou hast ordained, and beg Thee to treat me as a father has to treat his children! Here I am, Lord, to listen to Thee, and to obey Thee like a child!"

The second sentence: "HALLOWED BE THY NAME!"

This is the assurance of the worshipping soul as to how serious it is in everything it ventures to say to God. That it is with its whole intuitive perception with every word and thought, and does not misuse the Name of God through superficiality! Because it regards the Name of God as much too holy for that!

Consider, you who pray, what you are vowing with this! If you want to be absolutely honest with yourselves, you must confess that hitherto it is just with this that you men have lied in the Face of God; for you never were *so* earnest in prayer as the Son of God, in expectation, laid down in these words as a *condition!*

The third sentence: "THY KINGDOM COME!" is again no petition, but only a further vow! A declaring oneself prepared so that through the human soul life on earth shall become *such* as it is in the Kingdom of God!

Hence the word: "*Thy* Kingdom come!" This means: we wish also to develop so far here on earth that Thy perfect Kingdom may extend all the way to here! The soil shall be prepared by us so that everything lives only in Thy Holy Will, thus completely fulfilling Thy Laws of Creation, so that it will be *such* as is done in Thy Kingdom, the Spiritual Realm, where dwell the matured spirits who have become free from all guilt and burdens, who live only in service to the Will of God, because only in Its absolute fulfilment does good arise, through the Perfection inherent in It. Thus it is the assurance of wishing to become *such* that through the soul of man the earth also shall become a kingdom of fulfilment of God's Will!

This affirmation is further strengthened through the next sentence: "THY WILL BE DONE ON EARTH AS IT IS IN HEAVEN!"

This is not only the declaration of willingness to adapt entirely to the Divine Will, but also the inherent promise to trouble oneself about this Will, to strive with all one's zeal for the recognition of this Will. Indeed this striving must precede the adaptation to this Will; for as long as man does not know It aright he is not able to adjust himself to It either in his intuitive perception, his thoughts, words and deeds!

What appalling, punishable carelessness is it then for every human being ever and ever again to give these assurances to his God, while in reality he does not trouble himself at all about the nature of the Will of God, Which lies firmly anchored in Creation. Man simply lies with every word of the Prayer when he dares to utter it! He thereby stands before God as a hypocrite! Heaps onto old sins ever again new ones, and finally even feels he is to be pitied when he must break down ethereally under this burden in the beyond.

Only when these sentences are really fulfilled by a soul as a pre-condition can it then go on to say: "GIVE US THIS DAY OUR DAILY BREAD!"

That is as much as to say: "When I have fulfilled what I promised to be, then let Thy Blessing rest upon my earthly work, so that in attending to my gross material needs I may always have the time to be able to live according to Thy Will!"

"AND FORGIVE US OUR TRESPASSES AS WE FORGIVE THEM THAT TRESPASS AGAINST US!"

In this lies knowledge of the incorruptible, just reciprocal action of spiritual Laws that give the Will of God. At the same time also the expression of the assurance of full confidence in It; for the plea for forgiveness, thus release from guilt, is based *conditionally* on the *previous* fulfilment by the human soul of its own forgiveness of all the wrongs done to it by its fellowmen.

He who is capable of *that*, however, who has already forgiven his fellow-men everything, is also *so* inwardly purified that he himself will never *intentionally* do wrong! Therewith he is also free of all guilt before God, for there only all that is considered a

wrong which is done *intentionally from evil volition.*
It is only that which makes it a wrong. This is very
different from all human laws and earthly opinions
existing at the present time.

Hence the basis also of this sentence is again a promise before its God by every soul striving for the Light.
A declaration of its true volition, for whose fulfilment
it hopes to receive strength in the Prayer, through deep
absorption and becoming clear about itself; with the
right attitude this strength will also come to it in accordance with the Law of Reciprocal Action.

"AND LEAD US NOT INTO TEMPTATION!"

It is a wrong conception when man wants to read
into the words that he would be tempted through God.
God tempts no one! In this case it is only a question of
a doubtful tradition, which unfortunately chose this
word temptation. In its right meaning it is to be classed
with such concepts as going astray, becoming lost, thus
going wrong, seeking wrongly on the path towards the
Light.

It means much the same as: "Let us not take wrong
paths, nor seek in the wrong way, let us not take risks
with time! Waste it, fritter it away! But if necessary
restrain us *forcibly* from doing so, even if such a neces-
sity must strike us as suffering and pain."

Man should even gather this meaning already through
the following part-sentence, which according to its
wording indeed directly belongs to it: "BUT DELIVER US
FROM EVIL!"

The "but" shows clearly enough that they belong together. The meaning is synonymous with: "Let us recognise evil at all costs, even at the cost of suffering! Enable us to do so through Thy reciprocal actions whenever we err." In the recognising also lies the redeeming for those of goodwill!

With this ends the second part, the discourse with God. The third part forms the ending: "FOR THINE IS THE KINGDOM, AND THE POWER, AND THE GLORY, FOR EVER AND EVER! AMEN!"

As a jubilant avowal of feeling safe in the Omnipotence of God with the fulfilment of all that the soul lays at His Feet as a vow in the Prayer! –

This Prayer given by the Son of God thus has two parts. The introduction of approach, and the discourse. Through Luther there was finally added the jubilant avowal of the knowledge of the help for all that is contained in the discourse; of the receiving of strength to fulfil what the soul vowed to its God. And the fulfilment *must* then bear the soul upwards into the Kingdom of God, the Land of Eternal Joy and of Light!

Therewith the Lord's Prayer, if it is really experienced, will become the support and the staff for ascent into the Spiritual Realm!

Man must not forget that in a prayer he actually only has to obtain the strength to enable him *to bring into being himself* what he asks for! *So* shall he pray! And so too is worded the Prayer which the Son of God gave to the disciples!

CONTENTS

If you have questions about the content of this Work,
please contact Reader Services at:

Grail Foundation Press
P.O. Box 45
Gambier, Ohio 43022
Telephone: 614.427-9410
Fax: 614.427-4954